INTRO

We do hope you enjoy the book full of stories long and short.

You can read this book with your kid(s) or your kid(s) can read it by themselves. There might be some challenging words in the book in hopes the kid(s) or you can expand your vocabulary and make it a fun learning experience. Along with the opportunity to see things in different ways, and to help learn different lessons. All things in this book are fiction and is directed to be kid friendly.

TABLE OF CONTENTS

1 INTRO

2 TABLE OF CONTENTS

3-5 ADVENTURES OF MAX, BELLA, AND BUDDY

5-7 THE PURRFECT HALLOWEEN

7-9 HALLOWEEN HEROS

9-10 A GHOSTLY GATHERING

10-12 MILOS MIDNIGHT MUNCH

12-13 THREE LITTLE WITCHES

13-15 WEREWOLF BOYS ADVENTURE

15-16 PATCHY'S PUMPKIN ADVENTURE

16-17 THE GREAT PUMPKIN

18-20 HALLOWEEN OF THE FROG

20-23 NICK AND THE HALLOWEEN SUGAR MONSTER

23-25 THE FRIENDLY GHOST AND THE SPOOKY NIGHT

25-29 ZIGGLY-ZAGGLY AND THE HAUNTED HULLABALOO

ADVENTURES OF MAX, BELLA, AND BUDDY

In the heart of a bustling city, lived a pack of adorable dogs named Max, Bella, and Buddy. They were best friends, always up for adventures. When Halloween rolled around, the dogs were excited beyond belief. They loved dressing up in costumes and going door-to-door for treats.

On Halloween night, the dogs donned their costumes. Max was a brave pirate, Bella a graceful princess, and Buddy a mischievous ghost. They wagged their tails with joy as they set off on their Halloween adventure.

As they walked down the streets, the dogs greeted friendly neighbors and received a variety of treats. They had so much fun chasing after

falling leaves and playing with other costumed dogs. Bella, the princess, twirled in her sparkly dress, her crown sparkling in the moonlight. She was the picture of elegance and grace.

Buddy, the ghost, floated through the air, his white sheet billowing in the breeze. He was always up to mischief, and he loved scaring people.

As the night drew to a close, the dogs returned home, their bellies full of treats and their hearts filled with joy. They curled up together on the couch, dreaming of their Halloween adventures.

The next morning, the dogs woke up to a delicious breakfast. They had so many fun memories of their Halloween night. They knew they were lucky to have such a wonderful life filled with love, laughter, and adventures.

THE PURRFECT HALLOWEEN

In a small quiet town, lived a mischievous tabby cat named Oliver. He was always up to mischief, and Halloween was no exception. Oliver loved to sneak into people's houses and steal treats.

One Halloween night, Oliver decided to go on a trick-or-treating adventure of his own. He dressed up as a pirate cat, complete with an eye patch and a tiny sword. He crept through the neighborhood, his tail twitching with excitement.

Oliver visited many houses, and he managed to sneak a treat from each one. He was having a blast, but he knew he had to be careful not to get caught.

As Oliver was leaving one house, he heard a noise. He peeked inside and saw a little girl crying. Her favorite stuffed animal had gone missing.

Oliver decided to help the little girl. He searched the house, and he finally found the stuffed animal hiding behind a couch. He gently picked it up and returned it to the little girl.

The little girl was so happy to have her stuffed animal back. She thanked Oliver and gave him a big hug. Oliver felt warm and fuzzy inside.

From that day on, Oliver decided to be a good cat. He stopped stealing treats and started helping people. He even became friends with the little girl he had helped.

Oliver learned that Halloween could be about more than just trick-or-treating. It could be about helping others and spreading joy.

HALLOWEEN HEROES

Alex, Riley, and Ben, dressed as a superhero, a princess, and a ghost, set off on their Halloween adventure, eager to collect as much candy as possible.

As they explored the neighborhood, they stumbled upon a spooky-looking house with no decorations. Feeling a bit nervous, they approached cautiously, only to hear a faint cry for help.

Inside, they found Mrs. Willow, an elderly woman who had tripped and hurt her ankle. With bravery and kindness, the kids helped Mrs. Willow to her feet and called for an ambulance.

While waiting for help, they chatted with Mrs. Willow, learning about her life and the importance of helping others. When the paramedics arrived, Mrs. Willow thanked the kids for their heroism and gave them each a special treat.

As they continued their trick-or-treating adventure, Alex, Riley, and Ben realized that Halloween wasn't just about candy but also about helping others and spreading joy. They returned home with full bags of candy and a sense of accomplishment, knowing they had become real-life Halloween heroes.

A GHOSTLY GATHERING

In a quaint little town, Halloween was a time for spooky fun. The children eagerly dressed up as their favorite ghosts, monsters, and witches, ready to trick-or-treat and explore the neighborhood.

One evening, as the children were trick-or-treating, they stumbled upon an old, abandoned house. Feeling a bit scared, they hesitated to enter, but their curiosity got the better of them.

Inside, they found a gathering of friendly ghosts and monsters, all dressed up in their spookiest costumes. The ghosts floated around, giggling and playing, while the monsters danced and roared playfully.

The children were surprised to see that these creatures were not scary at all. They were friendly and welcoming, inviting the children to join their Halloween party.

Together, they played games, danced, and enjoyed each other's company. The children learned that ghosts and monsters were just like them, enjoying the fun and excitement of Halloween.

As the night wore on, the children reluctantly bid farewell to their new ghostly and monstrous friends. They left the abandoned house with hearts full of joy and a newfound appreciation for the magic of Halloween.

MILO'S MIDNIGHT MUNCH

Milo, a tiny mouse in a big city, loved Halloween. He would spend weeks planning his costume, scavenging for the perfect decorations, and dreaming of the delicious treats he would find.

One Halloween night, Milo decided to venture out into the big city, eager to explore and collect as much candy as he could. As he scurried through the streets, he noticed a peculiar glow coming from a nearby bakery. Intrigued, Milo crept closer and peered through the window.

Inside, he saw a table laden with delicious treats, all baked in the shape of mice! Milo's heart pounded with excitement. He knew he had to have some of those treats!

With a newfound determination, Milo squeezed through a small hole in the bakery's wall. He navigated the maze of shelves and counters, dodging the watchful eyes of the bakery's resident cat, until he reached the table of mouse-shaped treats.

Milo carefully selected a few of the most tempting-looking treats and tucked them into his little pouch. As he nibbled on his delicious loot, he couldn't help but feel a sense of accomplishment. He had not only found the perfect Halloween treat but had also embarked on a thrilling adventure.

As Milo made his way out of the bakery he got caught by the baker's cat. The cat told him it is not nice to steal things that don't belong to him, and Milo felt bad about what he had done. The cat said, "All you had to do was ask and we would have given you plenty of treats and goodies". Milo apologized for what he had done and the cat forgave him and told him to come back next Halloween. On Milo's way home he couldn't stop thinking about the bakery and the delicious treats he had been given. He knew that he would have to return there next year to see his friend the cat at the bakery and get more of those delicious treats.

THREE LITTLE WITCHES

Once upon a time, in a land of magic and mystery, lived three little witches named Willow, Hazel, and Ivy. They loved Halloween more than anything, especially the thrill of trick-or-treating.

On Halloween night, Willow, Hazel, and Ivy put on their most magical costumes and set off to explore the enchanted forest. As they wandered through the trees, they encountered a variety of spooky creatures, all dressed up for the holiday.

They met a friendly ghost named Jasper, who loved to tell spooky stories. They danced with a playful goblin named Twiggy, who played his magical flute. And they even had a tea party with a wise old witch named Grendel, who shared her secret spells.

As the night wore on, Willow, Hazel, and Ivy's bags were filled with treats and their hearts were filled with joy. They realized that Halloween wasn't just about candy, but about friendship, magic, and the joy of being together.

WEREWOLF BOY'S ADVENTURE

In the heart of the spooky Blackwood Forest, lived a young werewolf boy named Oliver. Oliver was different from the other werewolves. While they feared the full moon and transformed into ferocious beasts, Oliver loved it. He saw it as a time of adventure and transformation.

One Halloween night, as the moon hung high in the sky, Oliver couldn't resist the urge to explore the forest. He transformed into his werewolf form and set off on an adventure. As he wandered through the woods, he stumbled upon an abandoned castle.

Curiosity piqued, Oliver cautiously entered the castle. Inside, he found a hidden chamber filled with ancient artifacts and magical scrolls. He spent hours exploring the chamber, discovering secrets and learning about the history of the forest.

As he was about to leave, Oliver heard a faint whimper. He followed the sound to a small, frightened kitten trapped in a narrow passage.

Using his werewolf strength, Oliver carefully freed the kitten and carried it out of the castle.

The kitten, grateful for his rescue, purred contentedly in Oliver's arms. As they walked through the forest together, Oliver realized that even as a werewolf, he could be a hero.

When the sun began to rise, Oliver transformed back into his human form. He returned home with the kitten, which he named Luna. From that day on, Oliver and Luna were inseparable, and Oliver continued to explore the forest, always ready for new adventures.

PATCHY'S PUMPKIN ADVENTURE

Patchy was a pumpkin like no other. While his friends were content to sit on porches, waiting to be carved into jack-o'-lanterns, Patchy longed for adventure. He dreamed of trick-or-treating, exploring the neighborhood, and making new friends.

One night, as the moon hung high in the sky, Patchy's wish came true. He came to life, his stem wiggling with excitement. He rolled out of the pumpkin patch and began his journey.

Along the way, Patchy met a friendly ghost named Agatha, a mischievous goblin named Ryan, and a wise old witch named Blossom. They were all surprised to see a pumpkin come to life, but they welcomed Patchy with open arms.

Together, they explored the enchanted forest, played games, and shared stories. Patchy learned that even though he was different from his friends, they could still have fun and be friends.

As the hours passed, Patchy realized that his dream had come true. He had not only trick-or-treated but had also made new friends and experienced the magic of Halloween. As the sun began to rise, Patchy returned to the pumpkin patch, his heart filled with joy and excitement. He knew that he would never forget his incredible adventure.

THE GREAT PUMPKIN

Once upon a time, in a small town, there was a boy named Jack who hated vegetables. He loved candy and sweets, but he couldn't stand the sight or smell of fruits or vegetables. One Halloween night, he went trick-or-treating and ended up in a pumpkin patch.

A friendly ghost named Boo appeared and told Jack about the Great Pumpkin, who only visited children who ate their vegetables. Jack was disappointed, but he knew he wanted to meet the Great Pumpkin. Boo offered to help him learn to like vegetables.

Together, they explored the pumpkin patch and discovered a hidden garden filled with all kinds of vegetables. Boo showed Jack how to pick the freshest ones and taught him how to prepare them in delicious ways. Jack was surprised to find that vegetables could taste so good!

With Boo's help, Jack learned to make vegetable soup, roasted vegetables, and even a healthy vegetable smoothie. He was amazed at how much he enjoyed them. As Halloween night approached, Jack was ready to meet the Great Pumpkin.

On Halloween, the Great Pumpkin arrived and visited Jack. He was so impressed with Jack's newfound love for vegetables that he gave him a giant pumpkin filled with candy. Jack learned that eating vegetables wasn't so bad after all.

HALLOWEEN OF THE FROG

It was Halloween night, and the kids of Meadowbrook were ready for their biggest scare of the year. Every October, the town's massive corn maze, known as The Frightened Frog, opened for one night only, daring anyone to find the secret treasure hidden deep within its twisting paths. Legend had it, a magical frog once lived in the maze, and anyone who could find it would receive a year's worth of good luck.

Lila, a brave 11-year-old, had heard the stories her whole life. She had one goal this year—find the treasure and meet the magical frog. Along with her best friends, Sam and Emma, she entered the maze as the sun set, their flashlights beaming through the eerie stalks of corn. The air was crisp, and the maze was alive with the sounds of distant footsteps, laughter, and the occasional scream from a well-placed scarecrow.

As they wandered deeper into the maze, strange things started happening. First, their path seemed to shift, turning familiar routes into dead ends. Then, Sam swore he saw a glowing green shape hopping ahead of them, disappearing into the corn

"That has to be the frog!" Lila exclaimed, her heart racing. They followed the glowing shape, pushing through the maze's twists and turns, their excitement growing. Suddenly, they reached a large clearing in the center of the maze. There, sitting on a glowing pumpkin, was a frog—larger than any they had ever seen, with shimmering green skin and golden eyes that twinkled under the moonlight.

"You've found me," the frog croaked with a mischievous smile. "Not many make it this far."

Lila stepped forward, her hands trembling with excitement. "Are you the magical frog?"

The frog chuckled. "I am indeed. But I don't just give out treasure. You must solve my riddle first. If you succeed, the treasure is yours. If not, you'll have to wander the maze until sunrise."

Lila gulped but nodded, determined. The frog's eyes gleamed as he spoke:

"I'm light as a feather, yet the strongest can't hold me for long. What am I?"

The kids huddled together, thinking hard. Emma snapped her fingers. "It's your breath! No one can hold their breath forever!"

The frog's smile widened. "Clever girl! You've solved it!" With a flick of his webbed hand, a treasure chest appeared beside him. Inside, the kids found golden coins, sparkling candies, and a shimmering charm shaped like a frog.

"Take this charm," the frog said. "It will bring you good luck until next Halloween. And remember, the maze will always welcome those brave enough to seek its secrets."

Lila and her friends left the maze with their treasure and a story no one would believe. As they walked home under the stars, Lila couldn't help but smile, knowing they'd be back next year for another magical adventure.

NICK AND THE HALLOWEEN SUGAR MONSTER

Once upon a spooky Halloween night, a boy named Nick was excited beyond belief. Halloween was his favorite time of year, mainly because it meant one thing: candy. This year, Nick was determined to collect more sweets than ever before. He had a big pillowcase ready and a map of all the houses that gave out the best treats.

Dressed as a brave pirate, Nick set off into the night, going door to door with his friends. They raced from house to house, laughing and shouting, "Trick or treat!" Their bags grew heavier with every stop.

But while his friends were satisfied with their half-filled bags, Nick wasn't. He wanted more. He didn't care that his legs were getting tired, or that his stomach was rumbling from the mountain of candy he had already eaten. All Nick could think about was how much candy he could collect and eat.

As the moon climbed higher in the sky, Nick found himself at the edge of town, standing before an old, crooked house that looked like it belonged in a ghost story. A flickering jack-o'-lantern sat on the porch, and the windows glowed with a strange green light.

"This is where I'll get the best candy," Nick thought. He knocked on the door, expecting to see a friendly neighbor handing out chocolate bars. Instead, the door creaked open on its own, and a deep voice echoed from inside.

"Enter, brave one. The sweetest of treats await you."

Nick's curiosity got the better of him. Without hesitation, he stepped inside.

The house was filled with candy—more candy than Nick had ever seen in his life. There were mountains of chocolate, rivers of caramel, and clouds of cotton candy. In the middle of it all stood a figure dressed in a long, tattered cloak, its face hidden in shadow. It held out a bowl brimming with the biggest, juiciest candy Nick had ever laid eyes on.

"Eat all you want," the figure whispered, "but be warned, there is a price."

Nick, too excited to care, grabbed a handful and began eating. With every bite, the candy tasted more delicious, and soon, he couldn't stop. He stuffed his mouth with more and more, ignoring the warning.

But then, something strange happened.

His stomach started to growl—not the kind of growl from hunger, but from pain. Nick clutched his belly, feeling it swell like a balloon. He tried to stop eating, but his hands seemed to have a mind of their own, reaching for more candy, even though his body screamed for him to stop.

Suddenly, the figure threw back its hood, revealing a terrifying face made entirely of candy—gumdrop eyes, licorice hair, and a jaw full of razor-sharp candy corn teeth.

"I warned you!" it cackled. "Too much candy turns you into a Sugar Monster!"

Nick's reflection in a nearby mirror showed his skin turning sugary and his body bloating with sweets. He tried to scream, but all that came out were fizzy bubbles of soda pop.

Desperate to escape, Nick ran out of the house, but the Sugar Monster followed him, laughing maniacally. As Nick sprinted down the street, he felt himself getting slower and heavier, weighed down by all the sugar he had consumed.

Just when he thought he was doomed to become a sugar-coated creature forever, Nick spotted his friends at the end of the block. "Help!" he shouted, but his voice came out in a syrupy slur. His friends saw him and rushed over.

"Nick, what happened?" they asked, wide-eyed.

"The candy—too much candy," Nick gasped.

Realizing the danger, his friends quickly came up with a plan. They dragged him to the nearest water fountain and made him drink gallons of water to flush out all the sugar. With every gulp, Nick felt a little lighter, a little less sticky, until finally, the sugar spell broke.

The Sugar Monster vanished into the night with one last angry roar, leaving Nick and his friends panting on the ground.

That night, Nick learned an important lesson: too much candy is never a good idea. The next Halloween, Nick still went trick-or-treating, but he made sure to share his candy with his friends and eat it in small amounts—just enough to enjoy the sweetness without turning into a Sugar Monster again!

And from that day on, whenever he saw a big bowl of candy, Nick always heard the faint voice of the Sugar Monster whispering, "Remember, there's a price for too many sweets."

The Friendly Ghost and the Spooky Night

It was a chilly Halloween night in the small town of Willow Creek. The moon was full, casting a silver glow over the pumpkins on every doorstep. Kids in costumes ran from house to house, collecting candy, laughing, and shouting, "Trick or treat!"

But up on the hill, in an old mansion surrounded by tall trees, lived a little ghost named Oliver. He was friendly and shy, and he loved watching the kids enjoy Halloween. He wished he could join them, but he was too nervous. What if he scared someone by accident?

One year, Oliver decided to be brave. He put on his favorite hat—a big, floppy one that used to belong to the house's gardener—and floated down the hill. As he got closer to the houses, he saw kids dressed as witches, pirates, and even a few ghosts. They didn't seem scared of each other at all! Maybe they wouldn't be scared of him either.

Just as Oliver was about to approach a group of kids, a loud howl echoed through the night. The kids stopped in their tracks, looking around nervously. Then, from behind a large oak tree, stepped a tall figure covered in shadows. It was the mysterious Spooky Shadow, the town's Halloween trickster! Every year, Spooky Shadow would play pranks, making candy disappear and scaring kids with harmless tricks. But this year, he seemed even spookier.

"Who's ready for some mischief?" Spooky Shadow said with a cackling laugh, tossing a handful of glowing, green powder into the air. The wind swirled, and suddenly, all the streetlights flickered and went out. The kids screamed and huddled together, their candy bags shaking in their hands.

Oliver knew he had to do something. He might be shy, but he couldn't let the kids be scared. Taking a deep breath (even though ghosts don't need to breathe), he floated closer, his hat bobbing on his head.

"Hey, Spooky Shadow!" Oliver called out, his voice soft but steady. Spooky Shadow turned, surprised to see the little ghost standing up to him.

"Who are you?" Spooky Shadow sneered. "A ghost trying to stop me? How silly!"

But Oliver didn't back down. "Halloween is supposed to be fun, not frightening. You're scaring the kids too much. Why don't we play a game instead?"

Spooky Shadow raised an eyebrow, curious. "A game? What kind of game?"

Oliver floated closer and smiled. "How about a candy hunt? You hide the candy around the neighborhood, and we'll all search for it. Whoever finds the most gets a prize."

The kids, who had been watching from a distance, started to perk up. "Yeah! A candy hunt sounds fun!" one of them shouted.

Spooky Shadow thought for a moment, then nodded. "Alright, little ghost. You've got yourself a deal. But I'll hide the candy in the spookiest places. Let's see if you're brave enough to find it!"

With a flick of his wrist, Spooky Shadow sent the candy flying into the air. It disappeared into bushes, trees, and behind gravestones in the nearby park. The kids, excited by the challenge, ran off to start searching.

Oliver floated alongside them, helping to spot candy in tricky places, like under a creaky old bridge and inside a hollow pumpkin. The more they searched, the more fun they had, and even Spooky Shadow joined in the laughter, forgetting about his pranks.

By the end of the night, everyone had a bag full of candy, and they all agreed that it was the best Halloween ever. Oliver, the friendly ghost, had not only made new friends but had also shown that even a shy little ghost could make Halloween brighter.

As the kids waved goodbye and headed home, Spooky Shadow gave Oliver a nod. "You're alright, little ghost. Maybe next year, we'll team up for more fun."

Oliver smiled and floated back up the hill to his mansion, his heart warm and happy. He couldn't wait for next Halloween!

Ziggly-Zaggly and the Haunted Hullabaloo

In the wild, wiggly town of Wobblewood, where the streets twisted like licorice and houses teetered on the edge of their foundations, Halloween was always a night of wild surprises. But no one, not even the oldest wizards of Wobblewood, could have imagined the chaos of *this* year's celebration.

At the very tip-top of Jellybean Hill, inside the Wonky Mansion, lived a peculiar little creature named Ziggly-Zaggly. Ziggly-Zaggly wasn't a ghost, goblin, or witch—he was a *Floopernoodle*, the last of his kind. With one eye bigger than the other, ears that flopped like pancakes, and a tail that zig-zagged in every direction, Ziggly-Zaggly was as strange as his name. But most of all, he was known for throwing the wildest Halloween parties in all of Wobblewood!

Every year, Ziggly-Zaggly would invite the most bizarre creatures to his Haunted Hullabaloo—a party so legendary, it was said that even the pumpkins would start dancing in their patches. This year, though, something unexpected was brewing.

On the morning of Halloween, Ziggly-Zaggly woke up with his usual excitement and began preparing for the party. He polished his bat-shaped disco ball, stirred his bubbling cauldron of marshmallow soup, and hung glowing jellyfish from the ceiling. But just as he was about to start making his famous *Pumpkin Pudding Poppers*, a strange gust of wind swirled through the mansion.

"Wooooosh! Pfft! Toodle-doo!" The wind babbled nonsensically, scattering Ziggly-Zaggly's decorations across the room.

"What in the twisty-turny world?!" Ziggly-Zaggly cried, chasing after the runaway streamers. He hadn't ordered any talking wind, and he certainly didn't like the idea of things blowing around his perfectly organized chaos!

Then came a knock on the door—*knock knock KNOCK!*—so loud, the whole mansion shook like a bowl of jelly. Ziggly-Zaggly's eyes widened. "It's too early for guests!" he muttered, straightening his crooked bow tie.

When he opened the door, there stood a tall, lanky figure wrapped in a cloak made of shimmering shadows. Its face was hidden, but from beneath the hood, a cackling voice said, "I am Glorfnak the Garglesnort, the Mischief Master of Midnight! And I've come to crash your Haunted Hullabaloo!"

"Crash it?!" Ziggly-Zaggly gasped. "Nobody crashes a Hullabaloo! It's supposed to be fun!"

Glorfnak's eyes glowed red beneath his hood. "Fun? Pfft! Fun is for the *Unspooky*! I prefer chaos, confusion, and a sprinkle of mayhem. Let's see how your party goes after I mix things up!"

Before Ziggly-Zaggly could stop him, Glorfnak twirled his long, pointy finger in the air, creating a whirlwind of enchantments that flew out the door and into Wobblewood. He laughed and vanished in a puff of green smoke.

Ziggly-Zaggly blinked. "Oh, wobbleberries! This can't be good!"

As the sun set and the Haunted Hullabaloo guests arrived, things got weird—*really weird*. First came Lumphry the Lumpy-Lumpkin, a talking pumpkin with arms and legs made of licorice. He waddled in, his usual smile upside down.

"I can't stop walking backwards!" Lumphry cried, stumbling into the punch bowl.

Next came Tootsie the Two-Tongued Troll, who accidentally brought her twin tongued trolls along, and they wouldn't stop singing opera—badly.

Then there was Wibblington Wobblepants, a jittery jellyfish-man who couldn't keep his jelly limbs from wiggling at double speed. "I can't stop dancing!" he yelled as his legs wobbled him across the room like a runaway spinning top.

Soon, the whole mansion was in chaos. The bat-shaped disco ball turned into a *bat*, flying around the room. The marshmallow soup bubbled so high it floated out of its pot and started bouncing around like a balloon. And the glowing jellyfish decorations began singing sea shanties, throwing off the party's spooky vibes.

"This is a disaster!" Ziggly-Zaggly cried, dodging a flying marshmallow. He needed to fix this *right now*, or the Hullabaloo would go down as the worst party in Wobblewood history.

Suddenly, an idea zig-zagged through his head like his wiggly tail. What if... he made the chaos part of the fun? After all, what's Halloween without a little madness?

Ziggly-Zaggly jumped onto the stage (which was now bouncing up and down on its own) and grabbed the magic microphone. "Attention, Wobblewood weirdos! The Haunted Hullabaloo has officially turned into the Whirly-Swirly Chaos Carnival! Let's make this the wackiest party ever! Who's with me?"

The guests, who had been dodging flying decorations and wiggly food, paused. Then, Lumphry the Lumpy-Lumpkin raised his licorice arm. "I'm in!"

"Me too!" shouted Wibblington Wobblepants, his legs still flailing.

With a cheer, the partygoers embraced the chaos. They turned the flying marshmallows into a game of catch. The opera-singing tongues became the main act of a wacky concert. And the runaway bat-shaped disco ball? It became the star of a brand-new dance move—the Boo-Ball Boogie!

Just as the party reached its wildest, Glorfnak the Garglesnort reappeared, expecting to see a ruined event. But instead, he found Ziggly-Zaggly and his friends laughing, dancing, and having the best time of their lives.

Glorfnak's glowing red eyes flickered in confusion. "Wait... this is supposed to be chaotic! Not... fun!"

Ziggly-Zaggly floated over, grinning from ear to ear. "Oh, it's both! Thanks to your little prank, this is the best Haunted Hullabaloo ever!"

Glorfnak scratched his head, a small smile creeping onto his face. "Well... I guess I didn't expect that."

From that day on, Glorfnak joined Ziggly-Zaggly's annual party, helping to create the perfect mix of spookiness and silliness. And every Halloween in Wobblewood, the town celebrated the weirdest, wildest, most wonderful night of the year—the Whirly-Swirly Haunted Hullabaloo.

The End.

We hope you enjoyed the stories as much as our kids do and learned a few lessons along the way.

Dedicated to Dawn and Dusk Broadwater.

Made in United States
Orlando, FL
15 October 2024